Believing in Reading

BY THE SAME AUTHOR

A Much-maligned Town: Opinions of Reading 1126–2008
Abattoirs Road to Zinzan Street: Reading's Streets and their Names
The Reading Quiz Book
The Holy Brook or The Granator's Tale: Map and Guide
A Mark of Affection: The Soane Obelisk in Reading
The Stranger in Reading edited by Adam Sowan

ALSO PUBLISHED BY TWO RIVERS

Broad Street Chapel & the Origins of Dissent in Reading 2nd ed
　by Geoff Sawers
Newtown: A Photographic Journey in Reading 1974 by Terry Allsop
Bikes, Balls & Biscuitmen: Our Sporting Life by Tim Crooks
　& Reading Museum
Bizarre Berkshire by Duncan Mackay
Birds, Blocks & Stamps by Robert Gillmor
Reading Poetry: An Anthology edited by Peter Robinson
Reading: A Horse-Racing Town by Nigel Sutcliffe
Eat Wild by Duncan Mackay
Down by the River: The Thames and Kennet in Reading by Gillian Clark
From the Abbey to the Office: A Short Introduction to Reading and its Writers
　by Dennis Butts
A Ladder for Mr Oscar Wilde by Geoff Sawers
Roots and Branches: Battle & Caversham Libraries by David Cliffe
The Monmouth Rebellion and the Bloody Assizes by Geoff Sawers
A Thames Bestiary by Peter Hay and Geoff Sawers
Sumer is Icumen in by Phillipa Hardman and Barbara Morris
Charms against Jackals: 10 Years of Two Rivers Press edited by Adam Stout
　and Geoff Sawers
The Ancient Boundary of Reading [map] by Geoff Sawers and Adam Stout

Believing in Reading
Our places of worship

by Adam Sowan

TWO
RIVERS
PRESS

First published in the UK in 2012 by Two Rivers Press
7 Denmark Road, Reading RG1 5PA
www.tworiverspress.com

Copyright © Two Rivers Press 2012
Copyright © in text Adam Sowan 2012
Copyright © in illustrations Sally Castle (prints) and Martin Andrews (drawings) 2012

The right of Adam Sowan to be identified as the author of the work has been asserted by him in accordance with the Copyright, Designs and Patents Act of 1988.

All rights reserved. No part of this publication may be reproduced, stored in or introduced into a retrieval system, or transmitted, in any form, or by any means (electronic, mechanical, photocopying, recording or otherwise) without the prior written permission of the publisher.

ISBN 978-1-901677-84-3

1 2 3 4 5 6 7 8 9

Two Rivers Press is represented in the UK by Inpress Ltd and distributed by Central Books.

Cover design and linocut illustrations by Sally Castle
Pen and ink drawings by Martin Andrews
Text design by Nadja Guggi
Typeset in Bembo and Parisine

Printed and bound in Great Britain by Ashford Colour Press, Gosport

Contents

Introduction: a very potted history 1

The Minster Church of St Mary the Virgin, St Mary's Butts: a venerable vertical chessboard 5

St Laurence, Friar Street: geometry and youth at the Abbey gate 11

St Giles, Southampton Street: cobwebs and cattle pens 17

Greyfriars, Friar Street: multi-purpose survivor 23

St Mary, Castle Street: comings and goings in a classical context 29

Holy Trinity, Oxford Road: Brian's treasure-house 35

St James, Forbury Road: pre-gothic Pugin 41

The Sacred Heart, Watlington Street: save the rice pudding 47

Wesley, Queen's Road: oxen and honest brickwork 53

Friends' Meeting House, Church Street: Fox and Penn, Huntley and Palmer 59

Changing skylines: some suburban and ex-village churches, and places of worship for non-Christians 65

Afterword 71

Select bibliography 73

Acknowledgements

Thanks are due, as always, to the staff of Reading Library's Local Studies Collection; to Sidney Gold and Amanda Martin for help with particular queries; and especially to Chris Skidmore for much information about Quakers in Reading. We are also very grateful to the churches themselves for letting us in. Finally, I owe a huge debt to Sally Castle and Martin Andrews for their wonderful illustrations.

Introduction: a very potted history

The earliest evidence of Christianity in Reading was unearthed in 1988 by a man working in a gravel pit near Dean's Farm, Caversham. He broke into a well in which were buried the remains of a lead font or baptismal tank; it bore the Christian Chi-Ro symbol and dated from the 4th century AD, contemporary with the early church excavated at the Roman town of Silchester. There is little further trace of worship in the area until the year 634, when St Birinus arrived at Dorchester-on-Thames; he almost certainly sent priests out and about, some of whom may have set up some sort of church in Reading. In 979 it is believed by some that Queen Elfrida, having arranged the murder of her stepson Edward to ensure the succession of her full son Ethelred (later 'the Unready'), tried to atone for the deed by founding a nunnery in the town; it is not known for certain where this was.

The Domesday Book records one church in existence by 1086 (presumably St Mary's, now called the Minster), but hard facts on the subject really begin in 1121 with the founding of Henry I's great Abbey. The other two parishes, St Laurence and St Giles, were probably set up at about the same time, and served well enough for hundreds of years. Then, in the 17th and 18th centuries, came the rise of dissent and nonconformism, and a rapid increase in population in the 19th led to the creation of chapels-of-ease and the subdivision of the old parishes; there was a notable surge in church-building in the 1860s and 70s. Further growth in the suburbs before and after World War II brought a modest building programme, but in the 1970s declining attendances (and expensive maintenance bills) saw some Victorian churches demolished and others threatened; in 1971 Bishop Eric Knell said 'there are half a dozen churches in central Reading that we could do without'. Meanwhile, Roman Catholicism and some of the smaller sects flourished;

and non-Christian immigrants, needing their own spaces, made use of redundant churches and chapels as well as private houses.

There are now over 100 places of worship in Reading. I have given most space to ten with particularly interesting histories and/or architecture, and in telling their stories I have attempted to distinguish fact from tradition. Finally, this is not a treatise on comparative religion; having none myself, I have tried to write impartially.

Adam Sowan

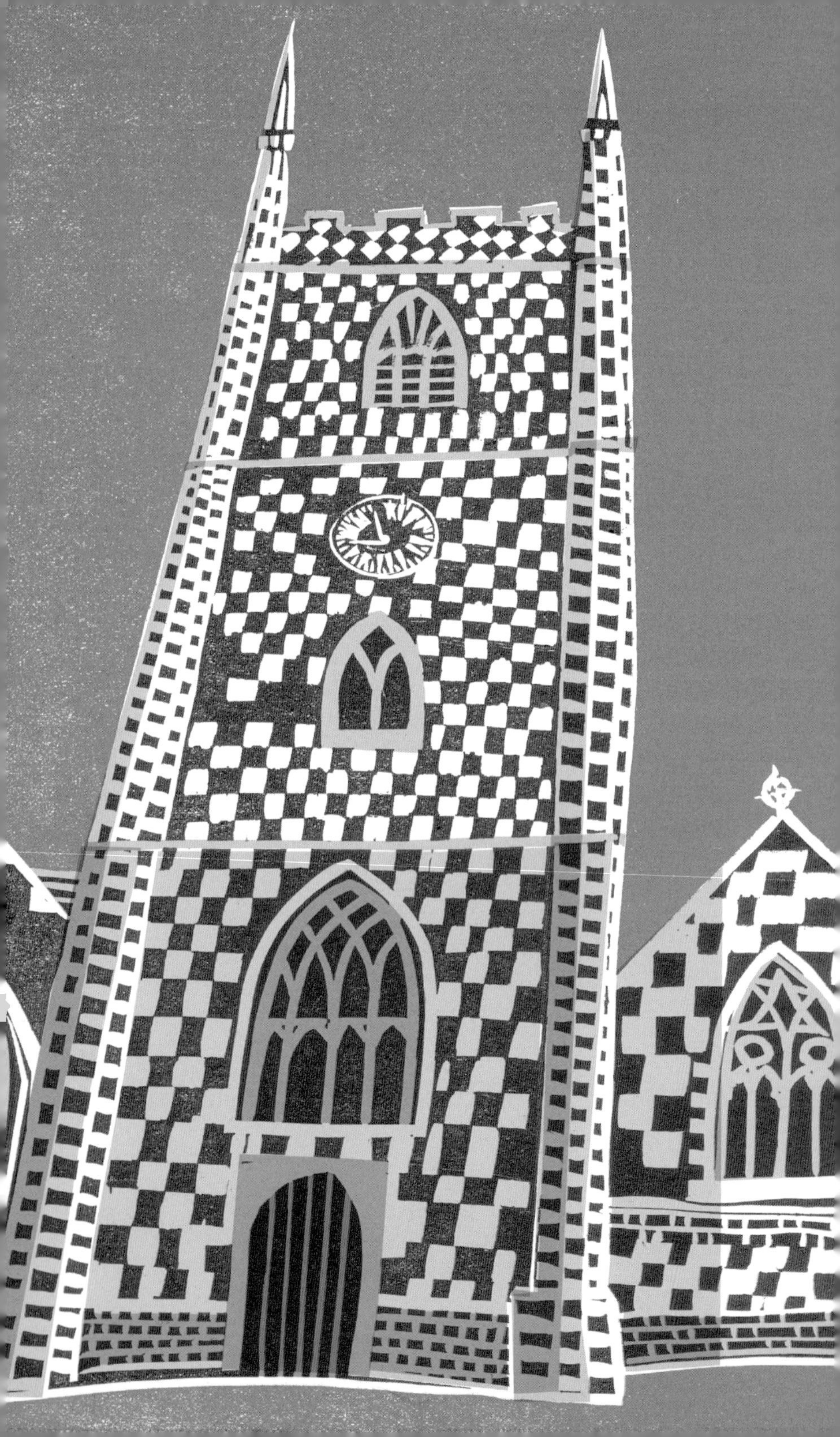

The Minster Church of St Mary the Virgin, St Mary's Butts: a venerable vertical chessboard

'this pretty, untidy, churchwardenised old church'

The word 'minster' is related to 'monastery', but over the years has been applied to a number of important churches with no monastic connection. It can be found in Victorian inscriptions in this church, and in 1877 someone complained about the usage in *The Reading Mercury*; but the word has been consistently used only since the 'millennial' celebrations in 1979 in connection with the nunnery mentioned in my introduction. It signifies that St Mary's is the town's principal church, where 'official' or celebratory services are held. There is no automatic link between city status and cathedrals; but if Reading ever becomes more than a town, the Minster might be a candidate for promotion.

The *Little Guide to Berkshire* (1934) said of the church that 'it has partly been rebuilt in modern times, with the result that its architecture is very queer and confused'. The oldest part of the present structure is a small Norman doorway in the north aisle, which looks as if it has been moved from somewhere else. Next comes the south arcade, which leans gently outwards and was probably built around 1173: the arches are still round, though the gothic style was advancing rapidly, and the capitals show a transition between two kinds of stylized foliage known to architectural historians as 'stiff-leaf' and 'waterleaf'. There were few changes over the next 350 years, apart from the addition of two chantry chapels in the 14th century. But in 1539, when the Abbey was dissolved, all three parish churches were stripped of their altars, statues, stained glass and other finery. On the plus side, plenty of stone was available from the Abbey ruins to effect a substantial restoration; a stone in the south porch records that 'this church was rebuilt in 1551'.

This included the building of the tower with its spectacular display of flint and stone chequerwork – which indeed covers most of the exterior, and looks particularly good after its recent repair and cleaning. The 18th-century diarist Mrs Lybbe Powis described the chequerwork as 'quincunx fashion', because the eye reads it in groups of five squares. At one time there was a timber spire, but it blew down in a storm in 1591. The tower houses a full set of bells, the heaviest in Berkshire; some of them date from 1640.

Reading's first historian, Charles Coates, wrote that St Mary's was 'repaired and beautified' in 1796, without specifying the work. The next major changes came in 1864 and 1872, when a new chancel and north aisle were erected. The chancel is in the Early English style, with simple, narrow, pointed windows. The aisle, paid for by local surgeon Isaac Harrinson, is 'Decorated' and was the work of the versatile and prolific Reading architect Joseph Morris. (A writer in the *Berkshire Archaeological Journal* in 1954 complained that 'this pretty, untidy, churchwardenised old church was viciously restored' under Morris.) Finally, in 1918, the early doorway to the north was opened out to give access to a new war memorial chapel; this is dedicated to St Edward, whose martyrdom may have prompted the foundation of the first church on this site (see Introduction).

Among the fitments and fittings may be noted the font, given in 1616 by the Vachell family and adorned with their coat of arms, along with those of their relations, the Knollyses and Reedes. The organ is by Father Willis, like the famous one in the Town Hall, but now in great need of repair and restoration. The splendid Jacobean monument on the north chancel wall is to William Kendrick, brother of John Kendrick who founded the Oracle workhouse across Minster Street. William, who died in 1635, was an early enthusiast for family history: the Latin inscription on the monument claims descent from a line of Saxon kings. A much later memorial in the Lady Chapel was carved by the noted English sculptor John Flaxman and commemorates John Monck (1809). The expiring Mr Monck, sitting in a chair, is fortified by a standing figure of Faith.

Font

One other intriguing feature is a wooden screen by the west door. Dated 1631, it sports some strange cloven-hoofed characters; some also have wings and some play odd musical instruments. The *Victoria County History* calls them satyrs.

Moving outside, the south wall bears a plaque recording the death of Laurenthes Braag in 1808. He was a young Danish merchant seaman caught up in the Napoleonic wars and billetted with many other prisoners of war in Reading. Among

*Cloven-hoofed, winged musician
above the west door*

the tombs in the churchyard, two groups of four are listed structures dating mostly from 1790–1830. The 1887 Jubilee Cross was designed by Slingsby Stallwood; English Heritage's listing citation says it was 'sited possibly as a reproach to the Jubilee Fountain' (in the middle of St Mary's Butts). There are some large and uncommon trees, including a Black Walnut, native to North America. The fruits are large and edible, but hard to crack. Better known are the Catalpa or Indian Bean trees near the west door. Some years ago the Council decided that the old twisty one (known locally as the 'trippy tree') had had its day, and turned it into a sculpture; but it refused to die, and sprouts happily alongside its young 'replacement'.

Until the late 19th century there were houses on the south and west sides of the graveyard, making it feel like a miniature cathedral close. The demolition of the Georgian vicarage in 1966 and the splendid 1840 Dispensary Trust in 1978 were great losses to the townscape, but the corner by Bill's Produce Store is still a quiet place.

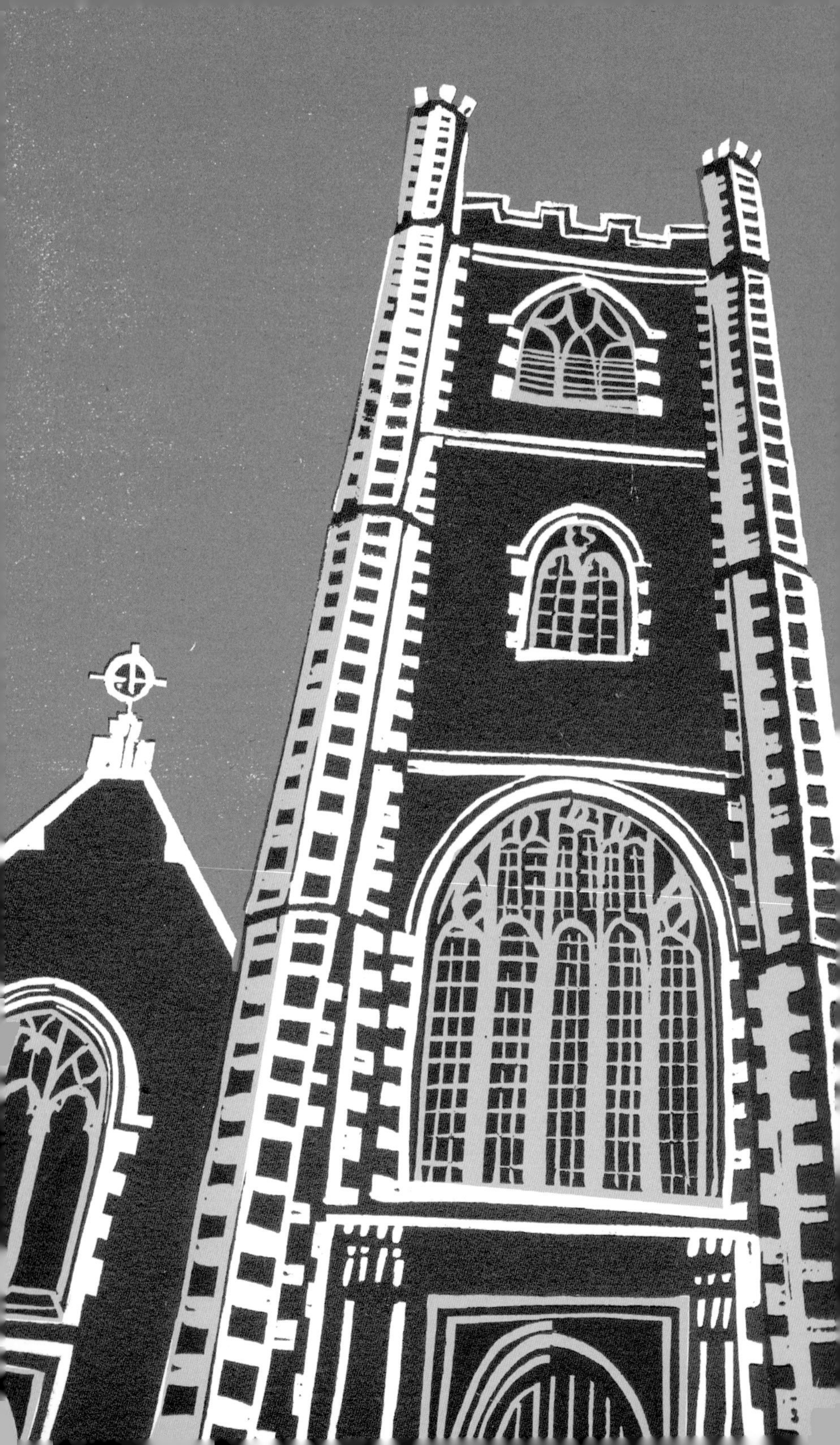

St Laurence, Friar Street:
geometry and youth at the Abbey gate

'paltry gingerbread ornaments of angels'

A timeline

258 AD — Laurence is martyred in Rome. Contrary to tradition, he was most likely beheaded, and not roasted on a gridiron.

c. 1121 — Reading Abbey founds a church for the townspeople next to the west gate of its precinct. The chancel and nave are, for some reason, not quite aligned.

1410 — The nave roof is built.

1450 — The tower, with its impressively tall arch to the nave, is put up. It now houses the only ring of twelve bells in Berkshire and is popular with campanologists.

1521 — The north arcade is erected.

1538 — According to Charles Coates, Reading's first historian, some frescoes are painted.

1552 — The font is installed.

1557 — The church claims its own set of relics. The list was much shorter than the Abbey's, but did include the obligatory piece of the True Cross.

1573 — William Laud, later a most controversial Archbishop of Canterbury, is baptised here.

1578 — The organ is taken down and sold 'for fear of the organ-takers'.

Lydall monument, 1608

ST LAURENCE

1611   The mathematician John Blagrave dies; his monument, on the south wall, carries five slinky ladies bearing the five regular solids in geometry, labelled Cubus, Tetrahedron, Octahedron, Dodicadron, and Isohedron (the sculptor's spellings).

1619   A renaissance-style six-bay covered way, at first known as The Walke but later The Piazza, is built against the south wall. Coates in 1802 calls it 'a handsome portico', but Man (1810) finds it 'a most clumsy and ill-formed arcade or corridor ... in defiance of every rule of architecture; a receptacle for idleness and vice, and where, I am told, midnight orgies are held'.

1719   A west gallery erected.

1727   A sundial is built into the south wall of the tower.

1741   A pulpit and organ case are installed.

1768   East gallery erected.

1789   *The Reading Mercury* prints a poem entitled 'On hearing Master Crotch play on the oboe in St Laurence's church'. Crotch went on to be a well-known organist.

1791   A stone on the east gateway of the churchyard proclaims 'enlarged anno 1791' – the gateway or the churchyard?

1802   Coates finds the roof 'very unsightly'.

1810   John Man criticises 'some paltry gingerbread ornaments of angels' by the west door.

1838   Dr Richard Valpy, long-serving headmaster of Reading School and 'mighty flogger', dies; his life-size monument glares down from the tower arch. He often preached in St Laurence's.

1840   Henry West, working on the almost-completed Great Western Railway station, is blown off the roof by a whirlwind; a memorial board can still be seen in the churchyard.

1846   William Poulton wins a competition to restore the church, but the Bishop of Oxford thinks his design 'not sufficiently consistent with the rules of ecclesiastical architecture'. Richard Billings and Benjamin Ferrey get the job.

1860 The public drinking fountain, with provision for dogs, is added to the south side of the tower. Its installation was prompted by the Drinking Fountains Association, founded the previous year to encourage supplies of clean water in public places. This one, the gift of Thomas Rogers, Clerk to the Board of Health, was designed by the architects William Poulton and Henry Woodman and has a beautiful carved relief of aquatic plants. An inscription, now worn away, read 'Fear of the Lord is a Fountain of Life'. Some members of the public worried that the fountain would become more a nuisance than a benefit.

Public drinking fountain, 1860

1867 More restoration.
1868 The Piazza is demolished by order of the Board of Health.
1922 The church's third rood screen is put up.
1943 The west window is blown out by a bomb. Its stone tracery was re-erected in the graveyard, where it remains to this day, weathering away.
1974 A scheme is mooted to convert the church to a museum.
2001 The parish is merged with the Minster and the building given a new purpose: 'living to see non-churched young people come to faith'. The pews were removed, and RRA Architects designed a steel-and-glass insert for the north aisle for meetings and catering; Pevsner calls it 'defiantly un-churchy'.
2004 Reading Borough Council announces plans to rebuild the churchyard wall, which had been propped up by scaffolding for ten years. It still is.

Though the general public rarely have access to the inside, St Laurence's contributes greatly to the townscape: the view from the Market Place has changed remarkably little in the last century. The churchyard provides a green and pleasant link to the Forbury Gardens.

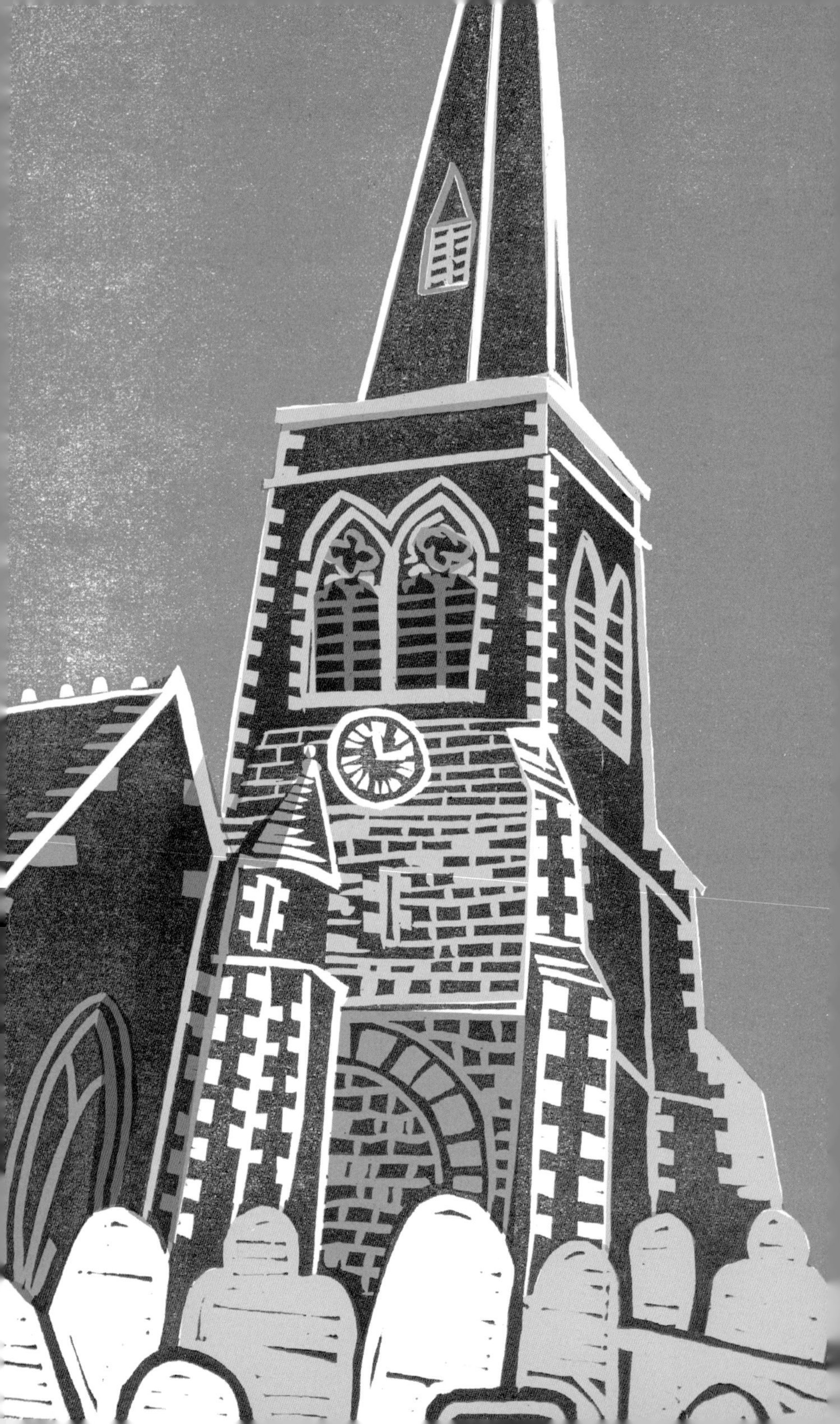

St Giles, Southampton Street:
cobwebs and cattle pens

'the finest old work in the town'

As with so many medieval foundations, the origins of St Giles's are obscure. But it probably started as a 'field church' or chapel-of-ease to St Mary's, serving the growing population that was beginning to spread south across the Kennet and up the hill to drier ground. It certainly existed in 1191, when the living was given to the Abbey along with that of St Mary's. When it became a parish in its own right it served an area of 2760 acres, stretching from the Kennet to the M4; it took six hours to perambulate the bounds in 1758. Most of it was outside the borough until 1887.

We don't know much about the shape and details of the original church: only parts of the outer walls and the base of the tower survive, along with a few carved stones that may have come from the Abbey. (Bits of Abbey can be found in old buildings all over Reading, mostly below ground level.) Leslie Harman, the assiduous historian of St Giles's and its parish, notes from the accounts and records that repairs and alterations were done in 1628, 1716, 1789 and 1822. The 1789 work was substantial, including the erection of a 70-foot spire of Riga Fir encased in copper, with a ball on top. This replaced a steeple that had been destroyed in the Civil War; it is said that in 1643 the Royalists planted a gun on top and the Parliamentarians blew it off. One commentator described the new one as 'a pretty little gothic affair'. The architect-builder (the jobs were not so distinct in those days) was one Henry Emlyn, who is best known for his decorative work at Windsor Castle. He apparently invented a 'British order' of architecture based on coupled columns which he called 'twintrees'; these terms never made it into architectural dictionaries.

As the population of the parish grew, furnishings multiplied, and a gallery on cast iron columns went up. Two retrospective descriptions from the 1880s give some idea of the interior: P.H. Ditchfield's *Ecclesiastical History* says 'it resembled somewhat the segment of an immense cobweb, of which a vast "three-decker" pulpit formed the centre. From this radiated with mathematical precision the pews …'. George Hillier's *Stranger's Guide to Reading* prefers 'an immense barn fitted with cattle pens'.

By the middle of the 19th century the congregation outgrew the church, and parts of the parish were hived off at various dates to form Christchurch at the top of the hill, St Stephen's in Newtown, St John's on Watlington Street, and St Luke's in Redlands. And in 1873 the mother church was almost entirely rebuilt, at a cost of £12,000, by James Piers St Aubyn. He wasn't one of the big guns of the gothic revival; mainly working in Devon and Cornwall, he also designed St Luke's and All Saints in Reading. All his churches have a strong individual character; here he chose the neo-gothic style of about 1250–1300, known then as 'Middle Pointed' but now referred to as 'Decorated'. Many of the windows have so-called 'geometrical' designs incorporating quatrefoils and trefoils within circles. The conspicuously slender stone spire is now tipping slightly to the south-west at the top. Inside, the chancel is particularly rich, with a fine reredos behind the altar. Few changes have been made since, so what we see now is something of an 1873 time capsule. Curiously, the *Little Guide to Berkshire* in 1934 claimed that St Giles's 'contains the finest old work in the town'.

Some monuments survive from earlier times, notably a brass of 1521 and some 18th-century wall tablets. One of these, on the east wall of the south transept and dated 1748, is the work of the renowned Flemish sculptor Peter Scheemakers; he did much for Westminster Abbey, including the Shakespeare memorial. One oddity is a plaque to a man who died 'on his way to the Bath', i.e. the big one in Somerset.

A church is, of course, more than its stones and contents; it is also the people who work and worship in it. To start with the dedicatee, St Giles himself: as with so many early saints,

Aubery monument by Peter Scheemakers, 1748

almost nothing certain is known of his life. He was apparently a hermit, and in due course became known as patron of the poor, beggars, the indigent and the distressed. This church has served its saint well over the centuries: it was at one time said to offer a higher-than-usual degree of sanctuary to those in need of it. During the Napoleonic wars it welcomed a number of French refugees, whose names can be found in the registers; in the 19th century it did a great deal of good work among the less fortunate souls who lived in the squalid courts and tenements off Southampton Street and Silver Street; and in 1962 the Reading Samaritans were based here.

Among the priests who have served at St Giles's, one of the more notable was John Eynon or Oynon, one of the English

Monument to John Eynon, one of the English martyrs

Martyrs hanged along with Abbot Hugh after the Dissolution of the monasteries in 1539; he was beatified in 1895. Others who need to be mentioned include a sequence of three influential preachers in the late 18th century: William Talbot, William Bromley Cadogan and Joseph Eyre. But their story will be found in my account of St Mary's, Castle Street.

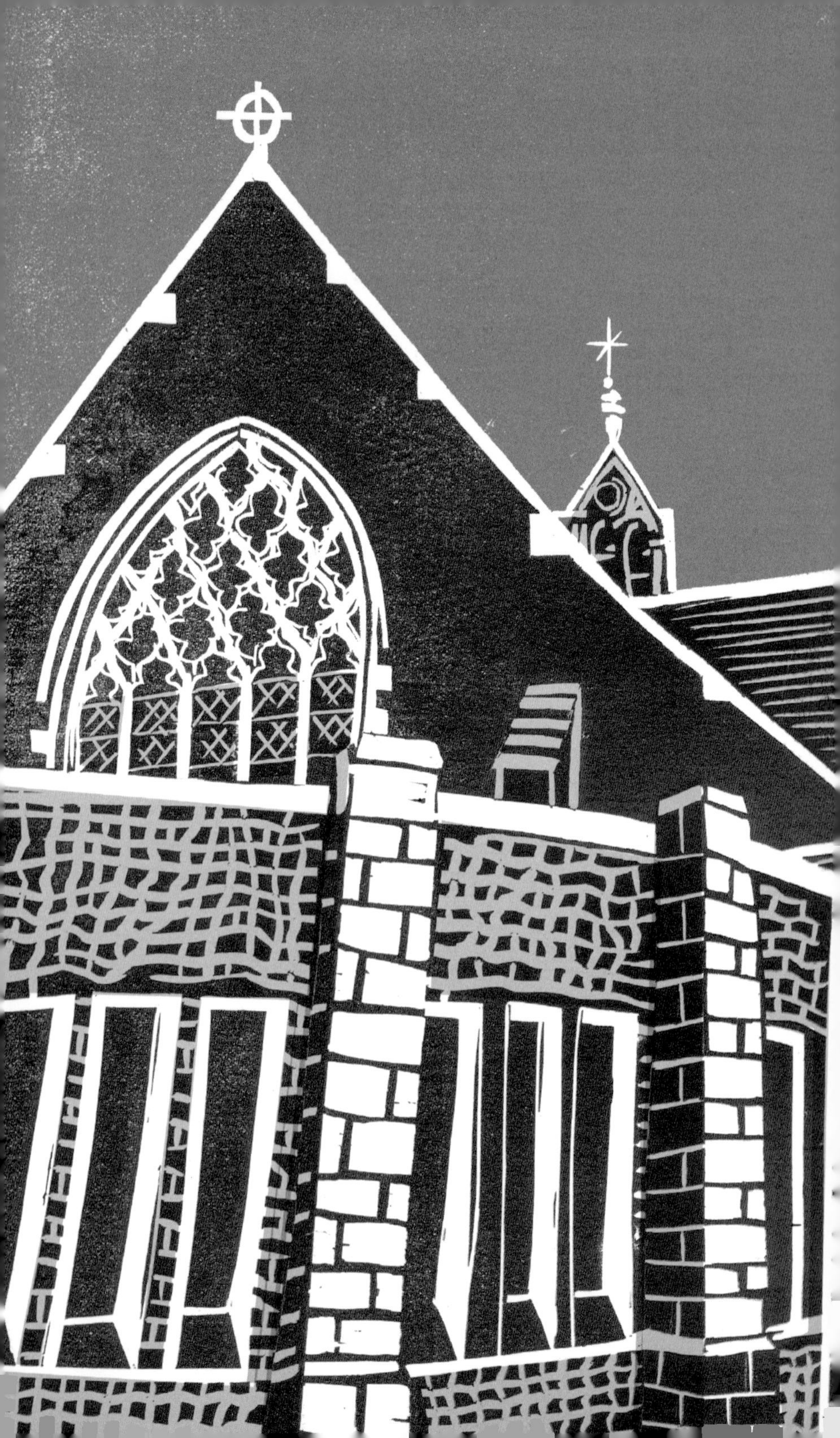

Greyfriars, Friar Street:
multi-purpose survivor

'this dismal abode of misery'

One of the carved angels on the font

In 1210 Francis of Assisi founded the order of Friars Minor, who chose a life of poverty and preaching in their distinctive grey habits. They soon reached England, and in 1233 the Benedictine Abbot of Reading granted them four soggy acres of ground near the Thames on which to establish a Friary, using wood from Windsor Forest. But the site proved too unhealthy even for ascetic monks, and in 1285 Archbishop Peckham, himself a Franciscan, persuaded the Abbey to give them the present site on higher ground. The new church, finished in 1311, was arguably the most elegant piece of architecture in town; its slim columns and arches were faithfully rebuilt 550 years later.

The Dissolution reached Greyfriars in 1538, the year before the Abbey. Much was destroyed, but five years later the Corporation took over the body of the church for a guildhall. Further changes of use followed: to a poor-house in 1578, a house of correction, bridewell or local prison in 1613, and (briefly) a guard-house during the Civil War. John Man's *Stranger in Reading* of 1810 paints a sorry picture of the wretched conditions suffered by the inmates. His final comment was a wish that some prison reformer, 'guided by humanity, might be tempted to visit this dismal abode of misery'. By the mid-19th century the building was roofless, dilapidated and threatened with demolition. Some archaeologists suggested converting it to a museum, but at the same time William Phelps, vicar of Holy Trinity, set in motion a campaign and appeal to restore it as an Anglican church. W. H. Woodman was engaged as architect, and it was reconsecrated in 1863. Much of the exterior flintwork is carefully cut or 'knapped' into neat squares.

There was little change in the next century, until in 1973 Greyfriars felt the need for a meeting room; within two years the semicircular 'West End' was built. At the end of the decade came a more ambitious plan for a larger hall on the site of the old church schools, and the Greyfriars Centre was duly put up, in a more contemporary style. The 1990s saw a re-ordering of the main church, with comfortable chairs replacing pews; in 2011 yet further extensions were proposed.

The neo-Georgian house next door at 64 Friar Street is now a day nursery, but when built in 1963 served as a replacement for a real Georgian vicarage. This started life in about 1800 as a home for Lancelot Austwick, Mayor of Reading. John Soane made drawings for Austwick, but the house as built was much simpler. The curved front garden walls may be attributable to Soane.

Greyfriars church today looks thoroughly Victorian, apart from the splendid reticulated west window. The inside is pleasingly plain and spacious, with a nave and (unusually for a Franciscan church) transepts. There is an immersion font, and on the wall a small display of old floor-tiles depicting animals.

Early 14th-century floor tiles

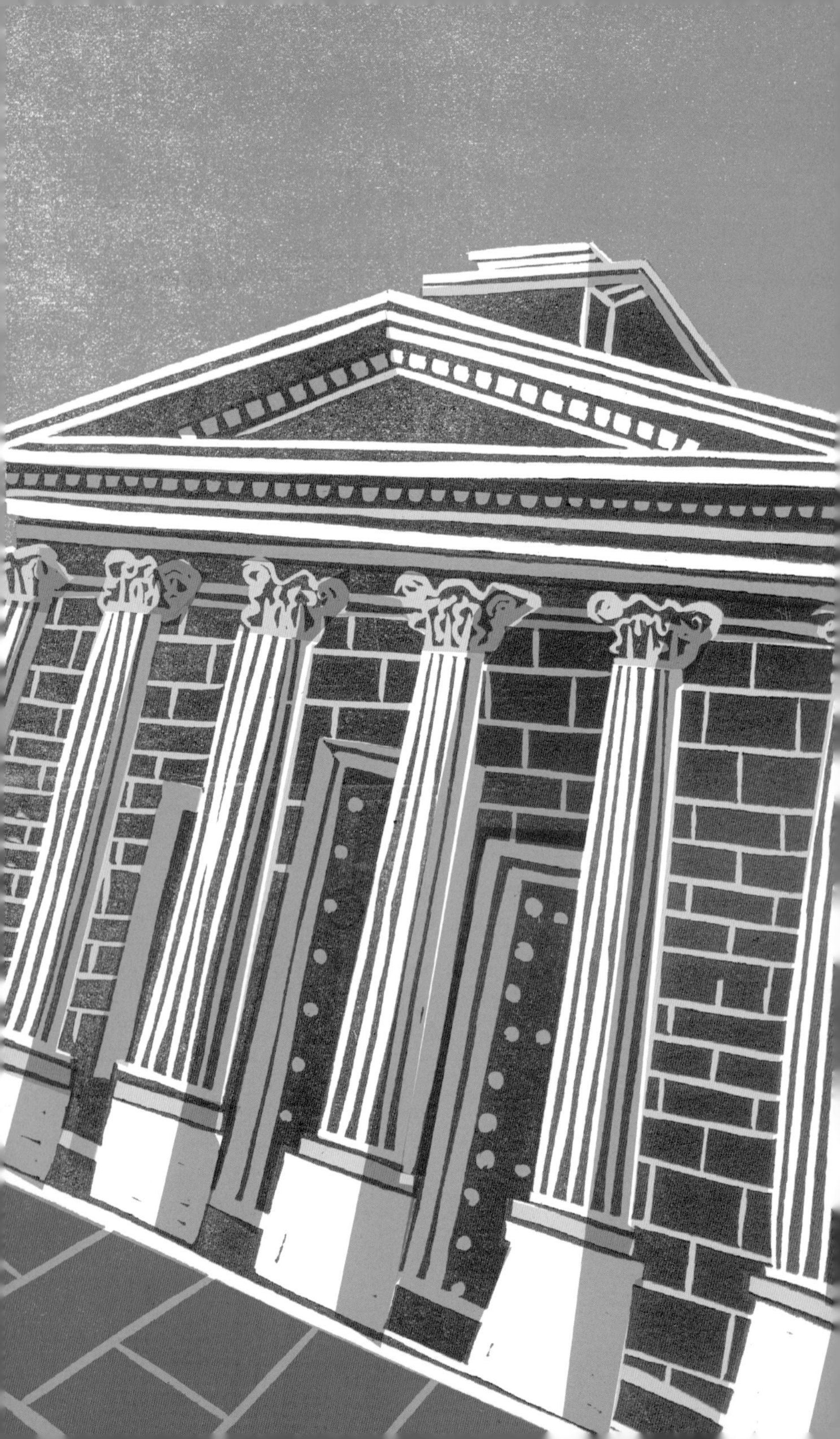

St Mary, Castle Street:
comings and goings in a classical context

'Tubbs's'

The 18th century was a time of religious change, perhaps more so in Reading than elsewhere. Many thought that the Church of England had become complacent and lost touch with ordinary people, and out of this dissatisfaction arose both Methodism and the Evangelical movement. Some talked of the 'Great Awakening'. Some Evangelical ministers were denied access to Church of England pulpits, but one who was allowed to preach in the new way was William Talbot, vicar of St Giles's from 1756 to 1768. On his death he was succeeded by William Bromley Cadogan, who did not, at that time, share Talbot's views. Many parishioners felt that they had to find a new place of worship, and help was forthcoming from that remarkable lady Selina, Countess of Huntingdon. At her own expense she trained priests at a college in Brecknockshire and built 64 chapels up and down the land: one of the best-preserved is in Bath, now open to the public as the Building of Bath Museum. In Reading she set up a small chapel in The Butts; but it was short-lived, because Cadogan came round to the Evangelical persuasion and the congregation returned to St Giles's. However, he in turn was succeeded, in 1797, by Joseph Eyre, who took very much the traditional line.

So the Evangelical party left St Giles's for a second time and returned to the Butts chapel, but not for long: very quickly they raised £2000 to buy the site of the old County Gaol in Castle Street and commissioned Richard Billing to design a perfectly square preaching-box to seat 1000 people. There was no chancel, and the street front was very plain and unadorned; called simply the Castle Street Chapel, it opened in 1798. The architect and his son, also Richard, did a lot of work in Reading, including Albion Place and Portland Place on the London Road – and the 1822 alterations to St Giles's. One of the most striking features of the Billings' interior is the galleries, which sit on iron columns with Doric and Ionic capitals, encased in plaster and covered with a very rare marble-effect wallpaper.

One of the early ministers was Henry Gauntlett, who took huge exception to Man's *Stranger*, which contained strictures on dissenters of all kinds. Gauntlett went so far as to put out a lengthy riposte; and yet he had already, in 1807, left Castle Street and returned to the Anglican fold. In 1821 the energetic James Sherman arrived; he oversaw the creation of five branch chapels in the environs of Reading, including the one at Caversham Hill which still functions. In 1823 the chandeliers at Castle Street were adapted for gas, which served until electric light arrived in 1900.

In 1836 there was a reconciliation with the Church of England, and the church was renamed St Mary's

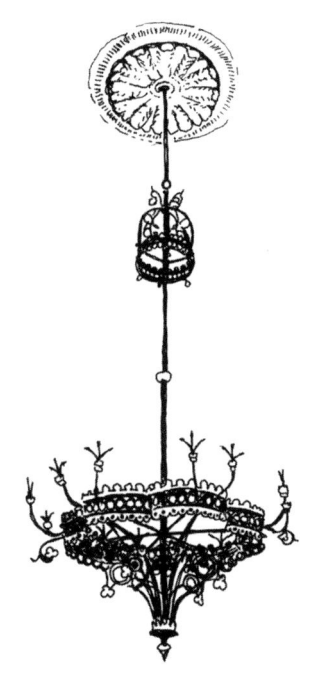

Gas-lit chandelier

Episcopal Chapel; it became a sort of chapel-of-ease, subordinate to the Minster, with no parish of its own. This change didn't suit everyone, and a section of the congregation split off and set up yet another chapel across the road. It kept going until 1956, latterly under the Congregational banner, and is now the Dogma nightclub.

Meanwhile, St Mary's underwent major physical changes. The chancel was added at the east end, and the magnificent classical west portico in 1840. This time the architect was Nathaniel Briant, another local man who, with his brother Henry, had built much of Eldon Road and Square. Nathaniel, alas, died in 1836, and Henry abandoned architecture to train for the priesthood. The stone columns of the portico have suffered time's ravages, but the Corinthian capitals remain crisp;

High pulpit

they are thought to be made of the artificial stone invented by Mrs Eleanor Coade. The new front is firmly fixed to the old fabric by two substantial iron tie-bars, the ends of which can be seen either side of the inner west doors. Above the portico stood an odd square bell-tower known as the pepper-box; some of its details were said to have been copied from the Tower of the Winds in Athens. It was taken down for safety reasons in the 1950s.

The church thrived in the latter 19th century, especially during the incumbency of George Tubbs (1853–88); indeed, it became familiarly known simply as 'Tubbs's'. A school was added at the back; the old box pews were cut down; the three-decker pulpit was replaced in 1860 by the present 'high' and 'low' pair, which Pevsner chooses to call 'elephantine'.

The 20th century saw many short-lived ministries and a good deal of debate about the church's future. At various times it was suggested that the site should be sold to pay for a new building, with its own parish, in the expanding suburbs – Southcote, Woodley or Caversham Park Village. The church did in fact do a lot of pastoral work in Woodley in the 1960s. But St Mary's had been listed in 1957, so could not be abandoned, though there was a proposal in 1973 to replace the unlisted eastern parts and schoolroom with a four-storey office block. The story of its survival is well told in John Dearing's history, aptly entitled *The Church that Would not Die*.

Since that book was published in 1993, the incumbent and the congregation decided that they could not in conscience continue in the ministry of the Church of England following the changes effected by the General Synod in 1992; so St Mary's is now part of the Church of England (Continuing), an association of churches committed to the traditional scriptural doctrines set out in the Thirty-nine Articles, to the Book of Common Prayer, and to an all-male priesthood.

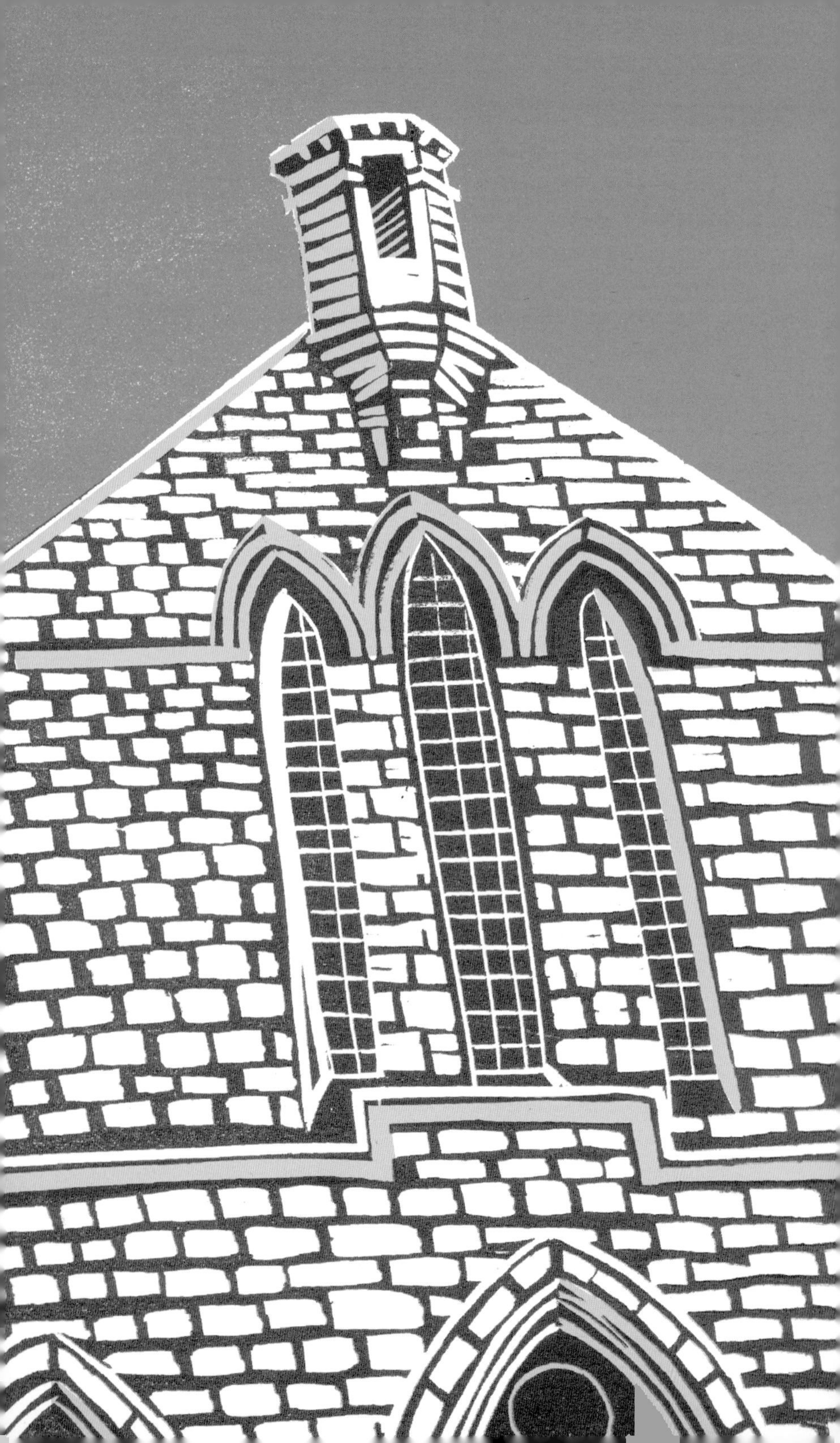

Holy Trinity, Oxford Road: Brian's treasure-house

'a gilded Anglo-Catholic confection'

Part of the Lady Chapel altar

An architectural enthusiast walking down the Oxford Road would hardly glance at this church's humble exterior, and might be surprised to learn that it is a listed building. As a proprietary chapel paid for by George Hulme, its first vicar, it was designed in the cheap, plain style known as 'Commissioners' Gothic' in 1826 by Edward Garbett, a local architect better known for his much showier church at Theale. Further funds were evidently available in 1845, when Reading architect and builder John Billing added a chaste stone front and a bellcote (which has since lost its conical hat). Shortly after this the church had the honour of being one of the very first to be photographed – by W.H. Fox Talbot, whose pioneering establishment was just up the road on Baker Street. In 1864 it became a chapel-of-ease to St Mary's in The Butts and six years later gained its own parish.

A century on, the transformation of the church to its present state began with the arrival of Canon Brian Dominic Frederick Titus Brindley (the second and fourth names were his own additions), and his taste and larger-than-life personality are evident as you go inside. Described variously as 'a bushy-haired Pickwick', 'a great epicurean', and 'the most impossible priest in the most impossible parish', he conducted – in the finest vestments – 'arguably the highest ceremonies in Anglican history', in which 'through clouds of incense, a liturgical *son et lumière* was performed'. His disapproval of the ordination of women led him eventually to go over to Rome; he objected to a new marriage service, arguing that the words 'that they might know each other with delight and tenderness in acts of love' would cause giggles in church. His death in 2001 was appropriately theatrical: celebrating his 70th birthday with many friends at the Athenaeum Club in London, he had a heart attack between the Latin grace and the dressed crab.

His legacy at Holy Trinity, which *The Spectator*'s obituary called 'a drab Victorian box transformed into a gilded Anglo-Catholic confection of gothic and baroque', is a collection of fixtures and fittings which – as Pevsner nicely puts it – he had 'garnered from redundant or unappreciative churches', and it is these that justify the listed status. From Oxford's All Saints and St Paul's came pulpit, altar, reredos, tabernacle,

Lectern

lectern and organ, mostly 18th century; there is also modern work, including a tall, thin aumbry by Martin Travers. But Brindley's prize acquisition was the rood screen thrown out in the 1960s by St Chad's Roman Catholic Cathedral in Birmingham, designed in 1840 by none other than A.W.N. Pugin, architect of St James's in Reading. Rosemary Hill's excellent biography of Pugin, *God's Architect*, recounts two things that resonate in Holy Trinity: firstly, Pugin, like Brindley, collected old and rare furnishings for installation in St Chad's; secondly, even as the cathedral neared completion, there was a heated debate about the merits of screens, with some churchmen arguing for an uninterrupted view of the chancel. Pugin prevailed, and his screen stayed, but only for 130 years.

A postscript: in 2011 Brindley's successor, Father David Elliot, resigned and led 15 of his flock to join an 'ordinariate' at St James's.

Section of the Pugin rood screen

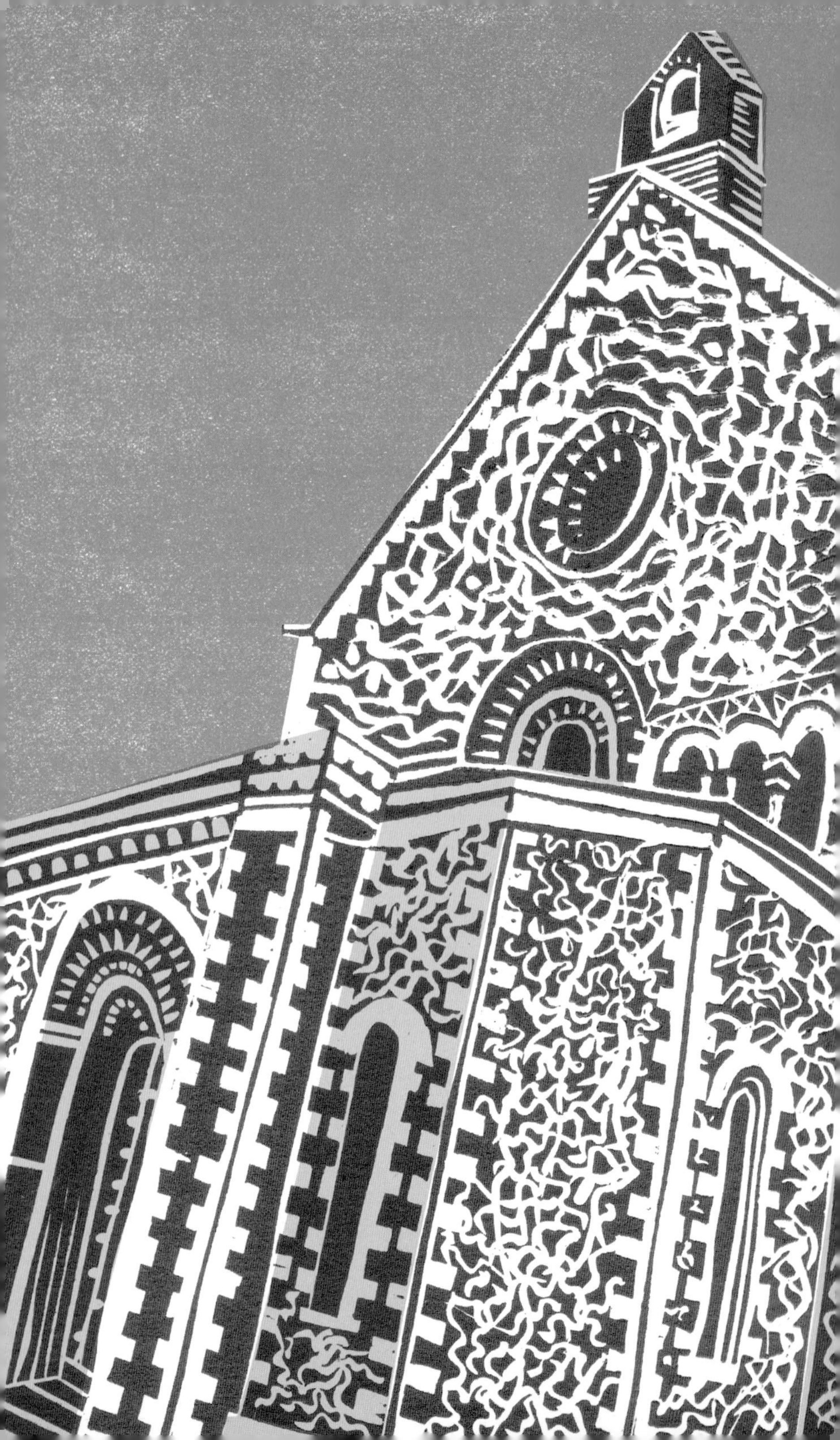

St James, Forbury Road:
pre-gothic Pugin

'Byzantine blossom'

The history of this building is very much bound up with that of Reading Abbey, which was founded in 1121 by Henry I. St James's stands within the precinct, next to a substantial chunk of the north transept of the great church, toppled by a mine during the Civil War. For many years after the Dissolution in 1539 the Roman Catholic faith was suppressed, though Mass was celebrated clandestinely in several local stately homes, including Mapledurham, Whiteknights, Stonor and Ufton Court. In 1706 there were 293 'papists' in Berkshire, and by 1741 there were said to be 300 in and around Reading. In about 1760 Anna Maria Smart, proprietress of *The Reading Mercury*, wife of the poet Christopher, and leader of the town's Roman Catholic community, rented a room in Minster Street for semi-public worship.

Things changed in the late 18th century with the passing of the Papists Act in 1778 and the Relief Act in 1791; the following year some 300 French priests arrived in Reading, driven out by the Revolution. The need for a church was met in 1812 by the establishment of the Chapel of the Resurrection at the other end of the Forbury, where the Rising Sun pub now stands; we do not know what this building looked like. By 1837 larger premises were required, and the antiquary James Wheble of Bulmershe Court bought and donated part of the Abbey site; he is buried in the cramped graveyard. The dedication derived from the Abbey's most famous relic, believed to be the hand of St James the Apostle; Reading was something of a mustering point for pilgrims bound for Santiago de Compostela. A mummified hand was found in the ruins in 1786, but there is no way of telling whose; it is now kept in St Peter's, Marlow, but occasionally exhibited in St James's on his feast day. Three of his trademark cockleshells can be seen carved in the apse. (The Abbey church itself was dedicated to John the Baptist and the Blessed Virgin Mary, not to James.)

The new church was a first ecclesiastical job for the young Augustus Welby Northmore Pugin, whose father was a French refugee. At the age of nine Augustus drew 'my first design', a crude elevation of a gothic church; by 25 he had decided that gothic was the one true Christian style. (He once mocked his own devotion to pointed arches: thanking a friend for the gift of a whole Cheddar cheese, he wrote 'while not strictly gothic in its present shape, it may be daily rendered more so by cutting it into four, which will make it a quatrefoil'. He was to have an enormous influence on the course of English architecture, though he died at 40, having destroyed his physical and mental health through overwork.

Here in Reading he chose, uniquely, the Norman or Romanesque style which, as Pevsner says, he would never have

Neo-Romanesque arcade

Font re-using stones from the Abbey

done even a few years later. One should not make too much of this apparent departure from his avowed preference: he was respecting the style of the Abbey, and indeed re-using some its stonework, and the result is much more pleasing than many neo-Norman efforts by later architects which tend to look ponderous and unconvincing. Furthermore, the word 'gothic' was used by Pugin's own father to include Romanesque. What he would certainly not have countenanced was a classical or renaissance design; his dislike of these 'pagan' styles and his open insults to the likes of Nash and Soane got him into trouble with the architectural establishment.

In 1838–9 Pugin designed 18 churches, two cathedrals, three convents, two monasteries, several schools and half a dozen houses, and cannot have spent a great deal of time on St James's. When it was consecrated in 1840 it was a single cell, with an apse but no aisles. The materials are local flint and sort-of-local Bath stone, which had been arriving along the Kennet and Avon since 1810 and is still dominant around the King's Road,

Eldon Square and the Royal Berkshire Hospital. The west front of the church, with its rich chevron decoration and round 'oculus' window, may have been inspired by the sumptuous late Norman example at Iffley, Oxford. In 1883 the organ and choir loft were added; in 1925 the architect Wilfrid Mangan designed the narthex or west porch, the south aisle or lady chapel, and the ambulatory running round the apse. Mangan respectfully stuck to Norman, though his other major work in Reading, the English Martyrs by Prospect Park, is a striking essay in the North Italian manner. Finally, in 1962, H. Bingham Towner contributed the north aisle, using functional octagonal pillars and domestic-looking Tudor windows that don't pretend to be Norman. The stained glass here, by Barbara Batt and Lynda Clayden, depicts St James, St Thomas Becket (who consecrated the Abbey), and Hugh Cook Faringdon, its last abbot. Two pieces of carved Abbey stonework can be found: the base of the tabernacle in the apse, and the upper part of the font; Pevsner praises its 'Byzantine blossom'.

For many years this building served most of Reading's Roman Catholic congregation, including a large influx of Irish after the troubles of 1850. This led to a certain amount of anti-Catholic feeling, which recurred in 1910 when Father Kernan staged a procession around the streets on Palm Sunday; this was declared 'illegal' and 'blasphemous' by the Protestant Alliance and others.

As the population continued to grow, a number of new parishes were set up in the suburbs after World War II. Around the same time, St James's welcomed an influx of Polish people, and a copy of a famous Polish icon, given by the Marian Fathers of Fawley Court, hangs in the south aisle.

The school next door was established by 1875, and took children of all ages until 1958; after spells as a primary and then an infant school, it is now a thriving day nursery.

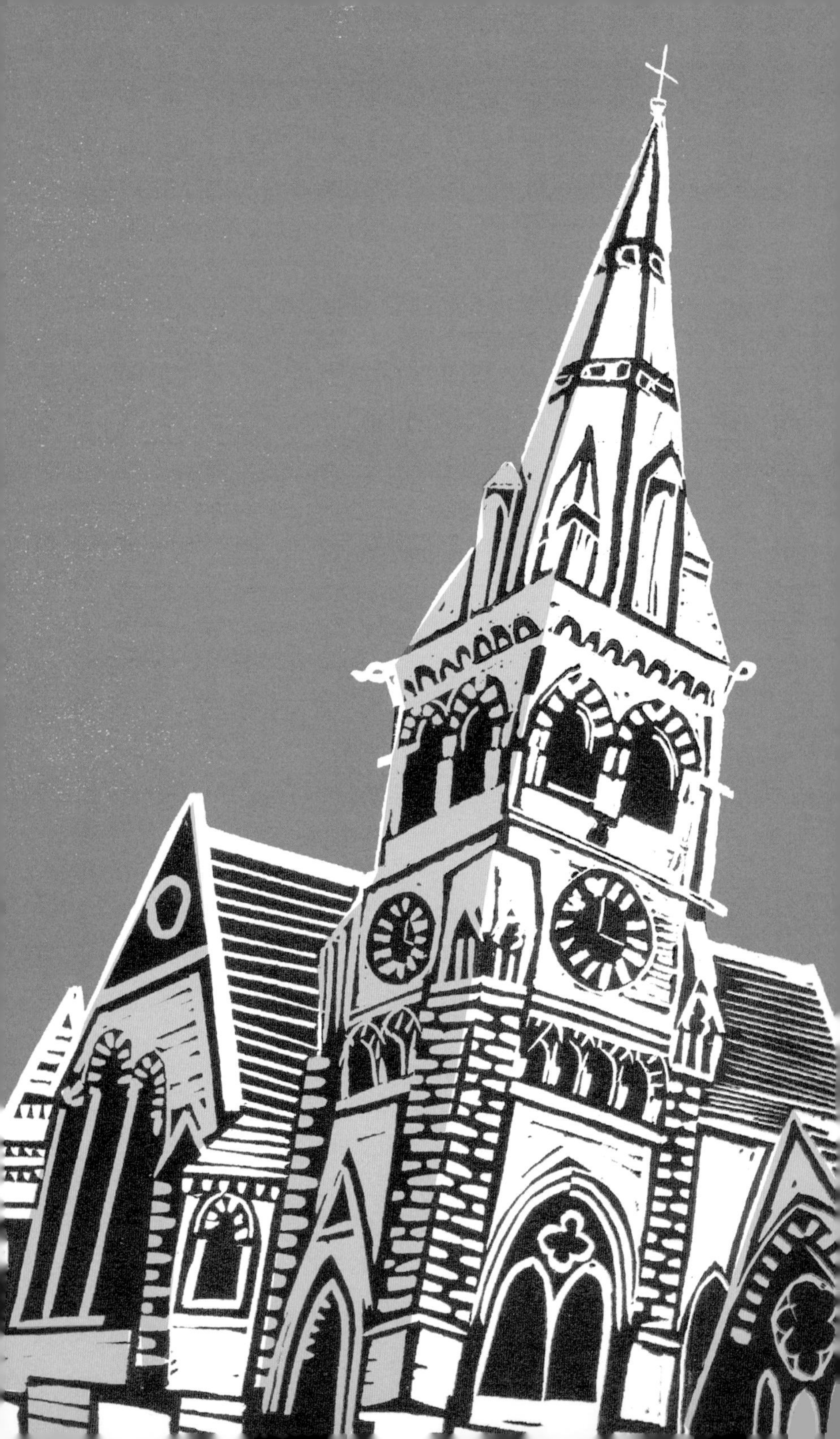

The Sacred Heart, Watlington Street:
save the rice pudding

'thick and curly'

Until 1981 this was an Anglican church dedicated to St John the Evangelist. In 1832 the Crown Lands that once belonged to the Abbey were sold off for building, and the rising population needed a church. In 1837 Francis Trench, curate of St Giles's, paid for its erection and engaged the architect Robert Ebbels of Wolverhampton. He designed a simple box with no aisles, in the style known as 'Commissioners' Perpendicular'. Someone called it 'a beautiful specimen of the rare gothic, exceedingly chaste of design'; and a new gothic church was indeed a rarity at that time.

The school next door was operating by 1854; in 1865, to celebrate the marriage of the Reverend Storrs, a grand party was given for the children, who were regaled with 40 pounds of cake and 15 bottles of wine. At about the same time the church acquired a new chancel, and some repairs were done in the next few years; but in 1871, when St John's achieved full parish status, the authorities decided to go for a new and larger building. One rejected idea was to move further down the King's Road to a site near Victoria Square, where Reading College is now. The architect this time was a little-known London man called William Allen Dixon. One of his few other churches still standing, a deconsecrated Congregational in Southend-on-Sea, is very similar, using mainly Kentish ragstone relieved by Bath limestone and red Mansfield sandstone.

Dixon could do neo-Norman and classical, but his style here has been described variously as Early English, 13th-century French, or Franco-Italianate. Whatever Dixon's intentions, it is unmistakably Victorian, as is the exactly contemporary, but very different, Wesley church across the road. On its opening in 1873 it was hailed as 'a handsome, spacious and well-lighted edifice'; H.S. Goodhart-Rendel, a specialist on the subject and period, praised it very faintly with a terse 'ordinary, not inexpert'; John Piper and John Betjeman said it was 'thick and curly'; and

Exterior window showing three kinds of contrasting stones

Reading's own H. Godwin Arnold found it 'muscular' but also 'not very interesting'.

The structure has changed little over 140 years. In 1884 an east window was installed in memory of Canon William Payne, a long-serving minister; there was some restoration, particularly in the chancel, by W.G. Lewton in 1897 and 1908; and in 1913 a new reredos was put up.

The story of the church's transition from Anglican St John's to the Polish Roman Catholic Sacred Heart begins in 1973, when the Church of England powers-that-were decided to merge the parish with St Stephen's on Orts Road, sell both sites, and build a new church in Newtown. Not much happened until 1978, when St John's was formally declared redundant and threatened with demolition. In August the vicar coined a possibly unique architectural epithet, calling it 'a good building, but not outstanding in quality; it is a rice pudding rather than fruit salad and cream'. There followed a long campaign to save it, supported by the local Residents' Association, Reading Civic Society and SAVE Britain's Heritage. Various compromises were proposed, including conversion to social housing for the

Squat columns illustrating 'muscular' architecture

James Butcher Housing Association, or just keeping the spire. The parish magazine referred to 'the exceptional deafness' and 'hectoring tone' of the objectors. A churchwarden wrote: 'To retain St John's would be a betrayal of our community'. Meanwhile, the large Polish Roman Catholic congregation in town, who were squeezing into St James's, offered to buy St John's. The Bishop of Reading wrote an article including the puzzling statement 'I was not ordained to become a museum curator'. He also asserted that 'the death [of St John's] must be a real death in order for the resurrection [of the new St Stephen's] in Orts Road also to be a reality'. There was a public enquiry; the case went to the Bishop of Oxford.

Although it was a listed building, as a redundant church it could be demolished anyway; but the churchyard wall,

One of the church banners bearing the Polish eagle

also listed, did not enjoy this exemption, and in December the Council refused permission to knock it down, making demolition of the church itself very difficult. Things dragged on until November 1979, when Archbishop Coggan, visiting Reading for the Minster's millennium, spoke to the campaigners. For whatever reason, early in 1981 the Church Commissioners had a change of heart and agreed to sell to the Poles, who re-dedicated and enthusiastically set about refurbishing it. In 2008 the Heritage Lottery Fund and English Heritage made grants for repairs and renovation, and happily this distinctive building, in the heart of a densely-populated and cohesive area that its historian Fred Padley called 'a village in the town', will be with us for many years to come.

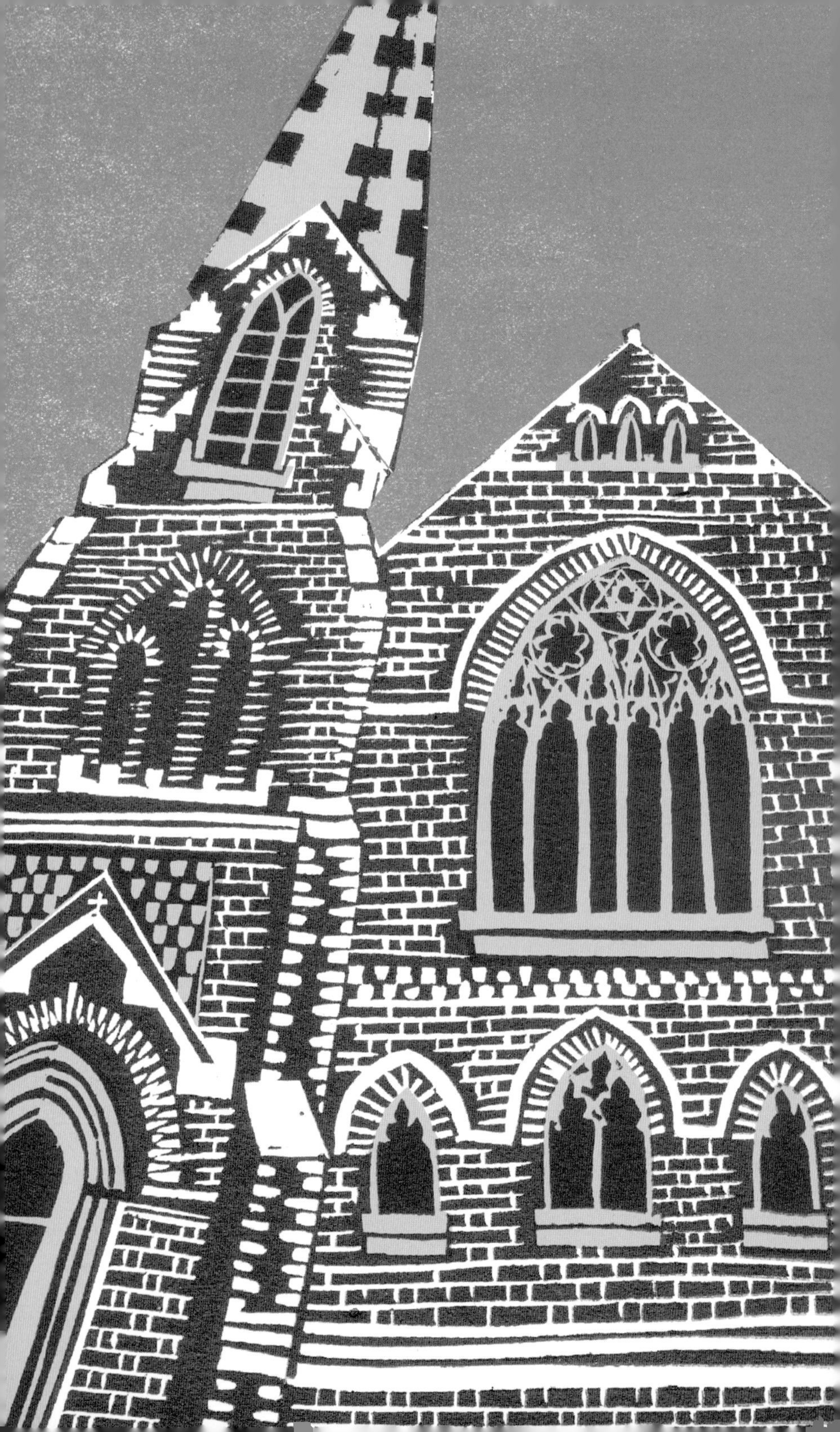

Wesley, Queen's Road:
oxen and honest brickwork

'a serious, well-behaved congregation'

The first Methodist Society in Reading was founded in 1739 by John Cennick, preacher, poet and hymn-writer. In that year John Wesley himself made the first of many visits, noting in his diary: 'I came to Reading, where a little company of us met in the evening; at which the zealous mob was so enraged, that they were ready to tear the house down'. In 1747 he preached to 'a serious, well-behaved congregation'; in 1755 he found them 'sleepy' and records that 'several soldiers were there and many more the next night, when I set before them the terrors of the Lord, and I scarce ever saw so much impression on this dull, senseless people'. But he was kinder to us in 1777, when he made the oft-quoted comment: 'How many years were we beating the air at this town? Stretching out our hands to a people stupid as oxen! But it is not so at present. That generation is passed away, and their children are of a more excellent spirit.'

Methodism seems to have faded from Reading by 1804, but in 1811 there were meetings in a passage off London Street, and then in a room in an old school near the present church. This temporary home, affectionately known as the Inkpot Chapel, lasted until the first purpose-built chapel went up off Church Street in 1817. This seated 550, and there were soon branches in West Street and in Spring Gardens up at Whitley Pump. By 1872 there was a need for a larger church to accommodate 900. The architect was nominally the Reverend J.P. Johnson, who had already designed what is now a Greek Orthodox cathedral on Trinity Road, Wood Green, North London; but in Reading he had professional help from the well-known and versatile Joseph Morris.

One of the principal indicators of architectural style is the design of windows and their tracery. In this respect this church is not unlike its neighbour and exact contemporary, St John's (now the Sacred Heart); but there the resemblance ends, largely because of the totally different choice of materials and applied decoration. Here we have local brick in English bond, mainly red with grey stripes and lozenges, and a slate roof: very much a product of Reading. The top of the white brick spire used to bear a weathercock, but it disappeared around 1960. Inside, we have elegant cast iron columns, delicate gallery-fronts, and a tiled frieze of lilies all around. There were few physical changes in the first hundred years: in 1899 Morris and Son added the manse, and in 1910 a vestry and lobby were designed by W.R. Howell.

A tiled frieze of lilies

Ceramic decorative panels mounted on the east end wall

The 20th century saw much extra-curricular activity: during the Great Depression the church organised Christmas morning breakfasts for children; by 1930 there was a Wesley Cricket Club, in 1946 a Dramatic Society; and in the early 1960s a Luncheon Club with visiting speakers, and a Youth Orchestra. As at St John's across the road, 1973 brought a threat to the church's future: the authorities considered replacing it with a smaller building. Another proposed redevelopment in 1993 also came to nothing, and by 1996 the congregation was raising funds to restore it to its present splendid state. The outside was cleaned (it had been hard to tell what colour the bricks were under decades of grime) and the sympathetic new entrance, meeting rooms and kitchen were added by the architect Ben Krauze.

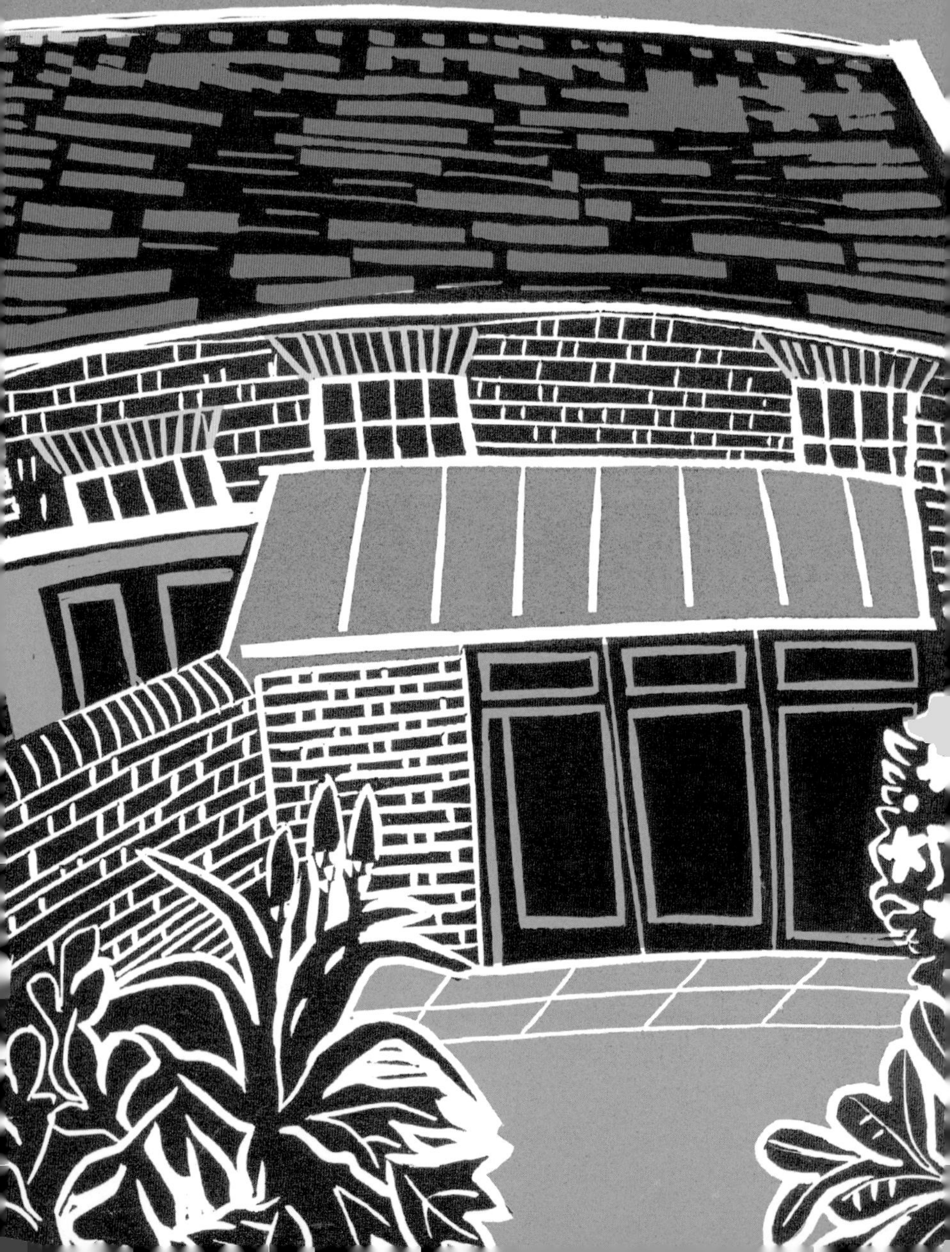

Friends' Meeting House, Church Street:
Fox and Penn, Huntley and Palmer

'a place kept tidy for the spirit of Jesus Christ'

The first record of Quaker activity in Reading tells us that early in 1655 Miles Halhead from Westmorland and Thomas Salthouse from Lancashire held three meetings: one at the bowling green behind the Broad Face Inn on the High Street, another at the Forbury, and the third at the house of Thomas Curtis in Sun Lane, where King Street is now. About three months later George Fox, founder of the Society of Friends, visited Reading and addressed a meeting in George Lamboll's orchard. His diary, written up some years later, notes that 'all ye whole tounde came together ... a glorious meeting it was & a great convincement of people there was yt [that] day: & people was mightily satisfied. And many baptists & ranters came privately after meetinge reasoning & disputing butt ye Lords power came over ym [them] all: & ye ranters pleaded yt God made ye Divell but I denied it ...'.

A view across the graveyard

It seems that the above-mentioned Thomas Curtis built the first proper meeting house in Back Lane, behind his house, in about 1671; it was probably a simple one-up-one-down building. Already, ten years before this, persecution of Friends had started with the passing of the Quaker Act in 1661. Many Quakers were imprisoned for disrupting church services or refusing to pay tithes; arrests were made at meetings in 1664–6, and three Friends died in gaol. In March 1664 Sir William Armorer JP came to the meeting in Curtis's house and arrested all the men. From 1 May he took the women as well; and on 22 May he came again 'with his usual Rage, but finding only a few Children and young Maidens in the Meeting, he struck one of them with his Staff, and ordered them to be pulled out, threatening to send them to Prison, if they came thither any more'. Charles II's Declaration of Indulgence of 1672 gave some relief, but sporadic persecution continued through the 18th century.

Meanwhile, internal Quaker schisms arose, in Reading and elsewhere, over the issue of separate business meetings for men and women. Curtis shut up his meeting house in 1684, and a few years later his opponents rented a tenement in Sims Court (the alleyway that still survives beside the RISC building on London Street). It was here that William Penn, founder of Pennsylvania, worshipped when living in retirement in Ruscombe. In 1705 he wrote: 'This is truly a town of meeting: of the waters of rivers, and of these friends in a place kept tidy for the spirit of Jesus Christ.'

Curtis died in 1712. In February 1747 the Quakers decided to buy some land that he had owned in Church Lane (now Church Street) for a new meeting house; simultaneously, moves were made to heal the schism. In 1715 the new burial ground was opened, replacing one in the vicinity of Sidmouth Street; still a peaceful oasis, it contains the graves of both Huntley and Palmer, founders of the great biscuit factory. Gravestones were not permitted until 1850.

In 1802 it was recorded that 162 dissenters and 12 Quakers resided in the parish of St Mary. John Man, in his *History and Antiquities of the Borough of Reading*, is less than kind: 'The quakers, as a sect, are the only ones among the dissenters at Reading, who appear to be on the decline. Education, that great polisher of human nature, may in some measure account for this change. The intellect, purified and enlightened, by the study of the best authors, among the ancient and modern writers, spurns at those fetters which the ignorance or fanaticism of former ages have prepared for it, and prompts the younger members of this religious society to rise superior to early prejudices, and boldly dare to think for themselves.'

The core of the present meeting house was built in 1835; typical of its age, its large windows provide plenty of natural light. The interior could be divided for segregated meetings by a sliding partition under a shallow arch. The stand at the east end, with sounding-board, was for recorded ministers. The foyer facing Church Street gained a surprisingly grand arched front in 1879; this was replaced by utilitarian extensions and alterations in the 1960s and 90s.

As well as Quaker meetings the house now hosts many activities: notably, the Liberal Progressive Jews meet here, as does the Reading Interfaith Group, in which individuals celebrate diversity and learn about each others' beliefs.

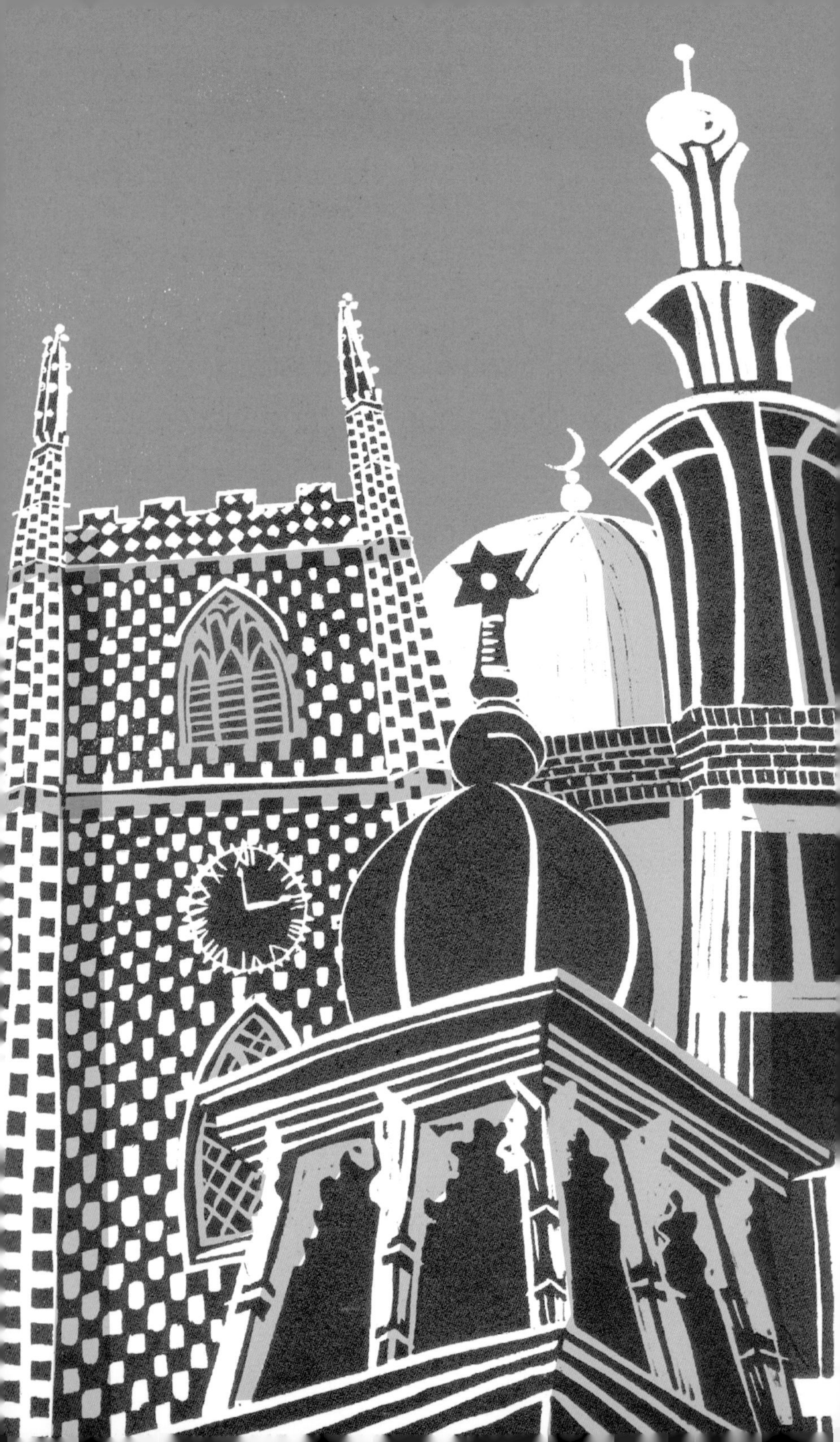

Changing skylines: some suburban and ex-village churches, and places of worship for non-Christians

'Let there be a variety of sects in the world'

'Let there be a variety of sects in the world'. John Man's plea will serve to introduce an account of some of Reading's off-centre churches, followed by a brief survey of non-Christian places of worship.

St Bartholomew, St Bartholomew's Road

As with so many saints, almost nothing is known for certain about Bartholomew's life, but legends are legion. He was believed to have been flayed alive, then laid in a marble coffin which floated around the Mediterranean for a couple of centuries. Most of him finished up in Rome, but a stray arm was brought to Canterbury by Cnut's Queen Emma; Sonning church once claimed to have his head. He was patron of bookbinders, butchers, cheesemongers, dyers, furriers, glovers, shoemakers, tailors, tanners, vinegrowers, slaves, poor people, and those with nervous diseases. The dedication of this church originated with the manor and chapel of Erleigh St Bartholomew (the other manor being Erleigh Whiteknights)

The nave, 1879, was the work of the nationally famous Quaker architect Alfred Waterhouse, he of Reading School, the south end of the Town Hall, and his own house at Foxhill, now on the University campus. This was one of his few church designs. The outside is local red brick with grey stripes. In 1902, when money allowed, G.F. Bodley, another big name, added a chancel (Waterhouse did not object); and in 1920 yet another well-known architect, Ninian Comper, designed a distinctive north-west porch.

The nave pillars are widely spaced; the narrow windows, with their tops partly hidden under shallow arches, are reminiscent of Waterhouse's work in the Town Hall. Carvings on the rood screen were made by a craftsman in Oberammergau, Bavaria. In the 1920s and 30s the church was quite High, and a 1959 guidebook makes much of its 'ornaments': altar frontals, candlesticks, lamps, aumbry, plate, censers, vestments. In 1978 the church was given permission to demolish its vicarage, also by Waterhouse, but thankfully this did not happen. In the 1990s St Bart's took two major steps: it merged its parish with St Luke's, and it welcomed two Orthodox congregations, first the Serbians and then the Greeks.

Christchurch, Christchurch Road

In 1860 the Reverend Thomas Fosbury of St Giles proposed a new parish with a church in a commanding position at the top of Kendrick Road. The subscription list featured many big Reading names, including Benyon, Blandy and Simonds. The architect was Surrey-based Henry Woodyer, and building proceeded in two campaigns, in 1861–2 and 1874–5. The spire is Reading's grandest; inside, Woodyer supplies plenty of quirky details, including nave capitals that one critic found 'difficult to accept as agreeable in an artistic sense'. But the most striking feature, admired by all, is the openwork reticulated tympanum in the chancel arch, no doubt standing for the Veil of the Temple. The old vicarage, now part of the Abbey School, is unmistakably by Waterhouse. The present congregation is very diverse, and has charitable connections with many overseas organisations.

St John, Woodley Green

Like Earley, Woodley was never a substantive place, but this corner retains a bit of a rural feel. The church, standing among great lime trees, was designed by Henry Woodyer (see Christchurch) and has his typically small windows, a French-looking bellcote, and a tall stone screen inside.

St Michael, Tilehurst

This parish once included the whole of Theale, and yet Tilehurst, as late as the 1879 Ordnance Survey map, was little more than the church, the school and the Plough Inn at what is now the Triangle. The tower, rebuilt in 1737, is of mixed red and silver-grey bricks, pleasingly random; the spire is nominally supported by vestigial flying buttresses; the body of the church, restored by G.E. Street in 1856, is done in carefully knapped (square-cut) flints. The main churchyard has a fine lime tree. In 2012, restoration work on the chancel floor uncovered the tomb of Henry Zinzan, of the local landowning family. Also buried here is Sir Peter Vanlore, a cloth merchant who hailed from Utrecht in the Netherlands. His showy monument proclaims 'When thou hast read the name "here lies Vanlore" thou needst no story to inform thee more'. But he goes on to praise himself anyway.

St Peter, Caversham

This church's Norman origins can be seen in the main doorway, one window, and the Purbeck marble font, which spent several centuries buried in the old rectory garden. Most of the structure dates from the 15th and 19th centuries. The original tower was another victim of the Civil War; its wooden replacement lasted until 1878. In the chancel is kept the wind-vane, dated 1663, from the gazebo by the Thames. The churchyard, dramatically perched above Caversham Court Gardens on a strong wall consisting of a series of concave curves, is steeply sloped. Among the big yew trees you can find an obelisk to the memory of William Crawshay, ironmaster and owner of Caversham Park.

St Peter, Church Road, Earley

Earley was not an old village, and has no real centre. This church started life as a chapel-of-ease to Sonning. It was largely paid for by Robert Palmer of Holme Park (no relation to the biscuit Palmers) and the Sidmouths of Erleigh Court. It was opened in 1844; the architect, John Turner, was employed by Palmer on his estate. The fabric is mainly grey brick with tinges of red; there are thin stone edgings, thin stone pinnacles, not-so-thin window tracery, and a big slate roof. In 1883 the church was considerably extended. Some frescoes painted in 1901 were covered up in the 1920s, not to be seen again until 1992.

Wycliffe, Cemetery Junction
For many years Reading's Baptists had a splendid neo-classical church of 1834 on King's Road, near the site of the present plain building on Abbey Square. It bore date-stones proclaiming 'Founded in Church Street 1640, removed to Hosier Street 1752; and to this spot 1834'. In 1978 the Borough Council were seeking ways to save it from demolition, to no avail. Wycliffe was built in 1887 as a daughter house; it is all brick, with a grey ground colour and red trimmings. It is relentlessly round-arched without pretending to be Norman; there are un-Norman classical pediments, strong horizontal bands, and a four-storey tower with an Italianish pantiled roof. The porch arcade, with fat pink granite columns and scroll capitals, looks rather out of place. The church runs Chinese and African Fellowships, and in 2000 it opened its well-used Warehouse community hall.

Other religions
In the 1880s, Reading's Jewish population, many of them tailors, began to organise themselves into a community, and at first held services in their own houses. As the century drew to a close, a big fundraising effort enabled them to commission local architect W.G. Lewton to design a synagogue to be built in what was then Junction Road, off the Oxford Road. The result was a striking mixture of Byzantine and Moorish motifs, notably including horseshoe arches over the main door and windows. On top, Lewton put a playful cupola with a star of David. The building opened on 31 October 1900; a cornerstone was laid by the Chief Rabbi and the foundation stone by a member of the prominent Goldsmid family. Sir Francis Goldsmid had been Mayor of Reading, and Junction

Road was renamed Goldsmid Road in his honour. World War II brought an influx of Jewish refugees, for whom temporary synagogues were set up in Tilehurst and Caversham. In 1979 a Liberal Progressive Jewish community was founded; they meet in the Friends' Meeting House.

The large local Muslim population has a number of premises around town: a mosque in a house in Alexandra Road (since 1976); another in a 1930s former Elim chapel in Waylen Street; and an Islamic Centre in South Street. For several years a purpose-built mosque in modern-traditional style, with minarets and a golden dome, has been going up on the Oxford Road; another was planned for Green Road in East Reading, but is unlikely to be built.

Buddhists have a Meditation Centre in one of the remaining Victorian mansions along the Bath Road; they also meet in Lower Earley.

In 1975 Reading's Sikhs converted a Victorian Primitive Methodist chapel in Cumberland Road, Newtown, to a temple or *gurdwara*; there is another on the London Road near the Suttons' Seeds roundabout. They spent ten years looking for somewhere to build a much larger one, and in 2012 submitted plans for a site on the Wokingham Road, near Earley station. It would have had two domed prayer halls and a contemplative garden with lotus pool. Their application has been turned down by Wokingham Council, and their search continues.

Since 1989 Hindus have worshipped in the former Methodist Hall at Whitley Pump. This was designed in 1905 by W. R. Howell, and Pevsner describes the façade as 'a reckless cocktail of 17th-century classicism and Tudor Gothic'. The main hall is very much intended to be used by local people; the temple itself is a smaller room at the back.

Afterword

I have tried to tell a story of growth and change in Reading's religious life; both of these processes will no doubt continue. The older churches are unlikely to be threatened with demolition, and more secular places will be adapted to faith use; indeed, as this book goes to press, the former Gaumont cinema is being converted from a snooker hall to a church. A rich variety of buildings will, for the foreseeable future, serve this happily multi-ethnic, multi-cultural and multi-faith town.

Select bibliography

Betjeman, John and Piper, John. *Murray's Berkshire Architectural Guide*. London: John Murray, 1949.

Brabant, F.G. *Berkshire* (Methuen Little Guides) 4th ed. London: Methuen, 1934.

Coates, Charles. *The History and Antiquities of Reading.* London: Printed for the author, 1802.

Dearing, John. *The Church that Would not Die: A new history of St Mary's Castle St Reading.* Baron Birch, 1993.

Ditchfield, P.H. ed. *An Ecclesiastical History of Reading: with a description of the churches, and a record of church work, by the clergy of Reading, and other writers.* Reading: E.J. and F. Blackwell, 1883.

Ditchfield, P.H. and Page, William eds. *The Victoria History of Berkshire.* London: Archibald Constable: St Catherine Press, 1906–1927.

Harman, Leslie. *The Parish of S. Giles-in-Reading.* Reading: 1946.

Hill, Rosemary. *God's Architect: Pugin and the building of romantic Britain.* London: Allen Lane, 2007.

Hillier, George. *The Stranger's Guide to the Town of Reading, with a History of the Abbey, etc.* 2nd ed. Reading: 1882.

Man, John. *The Stranger in Reading.* Reading: Snare, 1810.

Man, John. *History and Antiquities of the Borough of Reading.* Reading: Snare and Man, 1816.

Tyack, Geofrey, Bradley, Simon and Pevsner, Nikolaus. *Berkshire* (The Buildings of England). London: Yale University Press, 2010.

Two Rivers Press has been publishing in and about Reading since 1994. Founded by the artist Peter Hay (1951–2003), the press continues to delight readers, local and further afield, with its varied list of individually designed, thought-provoking books.